SPORTS CAREERS

by James Buckley Jr.

Minneapolis, Minnesota

Credits

Cover, © Harry How/Getty Images; 4, © DOD Photo/Alamy Stock Photo; 4–5, © The Bloomingtonian/Alamy Stock Photo; 5, © Steven Matto/Shutterstock; 6, © Chris Condon / Contributor/Getty Images; 7, © Paul Spinelli/AP Newsroom; 8, © Fabrizio Malisan/Alamy Stock Photo; 9, © Ramsey Cardy /Getty Images; 10, © Stan Szeto/Cal Sport Media/AP Newsroom; 11, © Andy Devlin / Contributor/Getty Images; 12–13, © Helge Prang/Verwendung weltweit/AP Newsroom; 13, © FatCamera/Getty Images; 14, © PJF Military Collection/Alamy Stock Photo; 15T, © Mykola Sosiukin/iStock; 15B, © Amar and Isabelle Guillen - Guillen Photo LLC/Alamy Stock Photo; 16, © Zuma Press, Inc./Alamy Stock Photo; 17, © Ronald Martinez/Getty Images; 18, © simonkr/iStock; 19, © Tribune Content Agency LLC/Alamy Stock Photo; 20, © Steve Jacobson/Shutterstock; 20–21, © Len Redkoles / Contributor/Getty Images; 22, © Zuma Press, Inc./Alamy Stock Photo; 23, © Gorodenkoff/Shutterstock; 24, © Fabio Pagani/Alamy Stock Photo; 24–25, © Ali Burman/Alamy Stock Photo; 26, © jacoblund/iStock; 27, © curved-light/Alamy Stock Photo; 28TL, © ultramarinfoto/iStock; 28TR, © wundervisuals/Getty Images; 28BL, © Ronald Martinez /Getty Images; 28BR, © Zuma Press, Inc./Alamy Stock Photo; 29, © ZUMA Press, Inc./Alamy Stock Photo; 31, © IlexImage/iStock; 32, © slobo/iStock.

Bearport Publishing Company Product Development Team
Publisher: Jen Jenson; Director of Product Development: Spencer Brinker; Managing Editor: Allison Juda; Editor: Cole Nelson; Associate Editor: Naomi Reich; Associate Editor: Tiana Tran; Art Director: Colin O'Dea; Designer: Kim Jones; Designer: Kayla Eggert; Product Development Specialist: Owen Hamlin

Statement on Usage of Generative Artificial Intelligence
Bearport Publishing remains committed to publishing high-quality nonfiction books. Therefore, we restrict the use of generative AI to ensure accuracy of all text and visual components pertaining to a book's subject. See BearportPublishing.com for details.

Library of Congress Cataloging-in-Publication Data

Title: Sports careers / by James Buckley Jr..
Description: Minneapolis, Minnesota : Bearport Publishing Company, 2025. |
    Series: Jobs on the edge | Includes bibliographical references and
    index.
Identifiers: LCCN 2024038093 (print) | LCCN 2024038094 (ebook) | ISBN
    9798892326513 (library binding) | ISBN 9798892326841 (ebook)
Subjects: LCSH: Sports--Vocational guidance--Juvenile literature.
Classification: LCC GV734 .B84 2025 (print) | LCC GV734 (ebook) | DDC
    796.023/73--dc23/eng/20240826
LC record available at https://lccn.loc.gov/2024038093
LC ebook record available at https://lccn.loc.gov/2024038094

Copyright © 2025 Bearport Publishing Company. All rights reserved. No part of this publication may be reproduced in whole or in part, stored in any retrieval system, or transmitted in any form or by any means, electronic, mechanical, photocopying, recording, or otherwise, without written permission from the publisher.

For more information, write to Bearport Publishing, 5357 Penn Avenue South, Minneapolis, MN 55419.

CONTENTS

Game Time! 4
Crunching the Numbers: Sports Data Analyst 6
Downhill in a Hurry! Downhill Skier 8
Good Luck Charm: Team Mascot 10
Getting Ready to Win: Athletic Trainer 12
Hold Your Breath: Free Diver 14
Sky-High on Wheels: Pro Skateboarder 16
Calling the Shots: Coach 18
Story Time: Sports Commentator 20
Touchdown! Pro Football Player 22
Under the Checkered Flag: Race Car Driver 24
Wheels for Miles: Long-Distance Cyclist 26
Your Turn! 28

Sports Career Spotlight: Mikaela Shiffrin 29
Glossary 30
Read More 31
Learn More Online 31
Index 32
About the Author 32

GAME TIME!

Whether on a field, a court, or even a snowy mountain, sports can entertain and inspire. Sports fans love watching the **pros** perform. But it takes many people on and off the field to make these moments possible. Let's explore some of the most exciting jobs in sports. Do you have what it takes to make the team?

Sports jobs are not just found in the pro **leagues**. There are even more of these jobs in high schools, colleges, and **amateur** sports.

CRUNCHING THE NUMBERS

Sports Data Analyst

When people think of sports, they may not think of numbers. But data **analysts** know numbers are a big part of understanding sports through math. These pros analyze every number, measurement, and **stat**, or statistic, they can. Then, the data analysts crunch these numbers to show athletes, coaches, and fans how well their teams are doing. Using this information, athletes can change how they practice and play to get better and better.

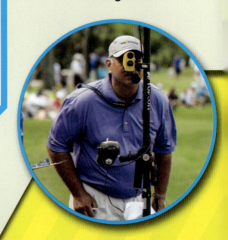

Some analysts use lasers to get information about golfers.

What It Takes

- ☑ A head for numbers
- ☑ Knowledge about athletes and teams
- ☑ An eye for patterns
- ☑ Communication skills

Sports data analysts can show which **plays** work the best for which teams.

The study of baseball stats is called sabermetrics. The name comes from SABR, the Society for American Baseball Research.

DOWNHILL IN A HURRY!

Downhill Skier

Downhill skiers zoom down snowy mountain courses with just two long and thin skis strapped to their feet. For the pros, it's all about the need for speed. Some skiers race straight down very steep hills. Others zip between trees or flags as they make their way toward the finish—it all depends on what type of skiing these sports workers specialize in.

What It Takes

- ☑ Balance
- ☑ Agility
- ☑ Many, many hours of practice
- ☑ Willingness to work in cold weather
- ☑ Quick reflexes

Slalom skiers move between flags in zigzags.

The top skiers aim to race in the World Cup or the Winter Olympics.

The fastest downhill skiers have reached speeds of more than 150 miles per hour (240 kph)!

GOOD LUCK CHARM

Team Mascot

Many sports teams have mascots, or characters who root for the team to get fans excited. These performers put on colorful costumes to dance, cheer, and interact with players. They keep the crowds entertained with funny acts between plays. Some people think a team's mascot even brings good luck. Go team!

What It Takes

- ☑ A sense of humor
- ☑ Dance skills
- ☑ Friendliness
- ☑ Creativity
- ☑ Being comfortable in crowds

Some mascots throw prizes to the crowd.

Mascots help fans cheer on their team.

Many people who work as mascots are **anonymous**. Their costumes cover their faces, so nobody knows who they are.

GETTING READY TO WIN

Athletic Trainer

How do athletes get so good at their sports? They have trainers to help them get ready to win! Trainers are sports experts who study medicine. They help athletes practice safely. Some trainers make workout plans to help athletes get stronger or faster. Others are on the field, ready at a moment's notice if an athlete gets hurt.

What It Takes
- ☑ A sports medicine degree
- ☑ Fast thinking
- ☑ Calm in a crisis
- ☑ Knowledge of sports

When athletes get hurt, athletic trainers guide their recovery.

Trainers show their athletes how to warm up for a workout to avoid injury.

Some athletic trainers help athletes plan and keep to a healthy diet specific to their sport.

HOLD YOUR BREATH

Free Diver

Free diving is a very challenging sport. These amazing athletes swim deep underwater with just one big breath. Some dive as deep as they can go, while others take the plunge to compete to see how long they can stay underwater. Only the most dedicated and highly trained free divers become champions of the sport. The rest of us know when to come up for air!

What It Takes

- ☑ Large lung capacity
- ☑ Courage
- ☑ Calm under pressure
- ☑ Strong swimming skills
- ☑ A sense of adventure

Some free divers play games, such as underwater football.

Rescue divers are ready with air tanks if a free diver needs help.

Some free divers have dived deeper than 660 ft. (200 m).

The best free divers can hold their breath for longer than 20 minutes!

SKY-HIGH ON WHEELS

Pro Skateboarder

Skateboarding is one of the gnarliest sports around! Many people skateboard, but pro skateboarders can do stunningly complex tricks. Sometimes, they fly off huge ramps and spin or flip in the air. Other times, they slide down a thin rail on their skateboards. It takes a lot of practice to do these difficult tricks without falling. But every pro skater who falls down gets back up to try again.

What It Takes

- ☑ Balance
- ☑ **Agility**
- ☑ Creativity
- ☑ A sense of adventure
- ☑ **Persistence**

Some skaters compete on high ramps.

Skaters wear helmets and pads to stay safe.

Skateboarding made its first appearance at the Olympics in 2021.

CALLING THE SHOTS

Coach

Every team needs a leader. In many sports, the coach is the head of the team. These dedicated workers are at every game, competition, and practice, pushing their athletes to do their best. Coaches come up with the best **tactics** to win. This means they have to watch other teams and learn how they play.

What It Takes

- ☑ Deep knowledge of the sport
- ☑ Leadership skills
- ☑ Good communication
- ☑ Listening skills
- ☑ Quick thinking
- ☑ Great organization

Coaches cheer on their athletes at competitions.

Coaches switch out players when teammates need a break.

Many professional teams have one head coach and several assistant coaches.

19

STORY TIME

Sports Commentator

Wait . . . what was that? Games can be fast and hard to follow. A sports commentator watches the game carefully. They describe what is happening to help fans keep track of the action. Sports commentators have to talk quickly so they can keep up with fast gameplay. Their love for the sport helps fans get excited, too. They tell stories about the teams and players so fans get to know their favorite athletes.

What It Takes
- ☑ A clear voice
- ☑ A journalism or broadcasting degree
- ☑ Multitasking skills
- ☑ Quick thinking

Sideline reporters are commentators who interview players on the field.

Sports commentators may sit in a special box above the action to see the game better.

Some sports commentators work on the radio. They describe what is happening to listeners who can't see the action.

21

TOUCHDOWN!

Pro Football Player

Football is a tough sport, and players in the **National Football League (NFL)** are some of the toughest. They need to be strong enough to tackle others to the ground and fast enough to escape the other team. With teamwork, they move the ball down the field and into the end zone. All of that skill takes a lot of practice. Football players train with their teammates for weeks before they face another team on game day.

What It Takes
- ☑ College football experience
- ☑ Strength
- ☑ Speed
- ☑ Teamwork
- ☑ Toughness

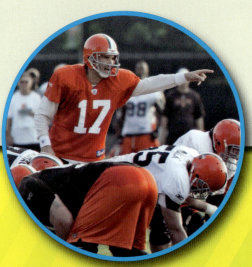

Training season is a time when football players practice with their team.

Each team gets four downs, or tries, to run the ball down the field. Then the other team gets the ball.

Each football team has two groups of players, an offense and a defense. The offense tries to run the ball into the end zone. The other team's defense tries to stop them.

23

UNDER THE CHECKERED FLAG

Race Car Driver

Zoom! Race cars zip around the turns of a racetrack. The people driving those cars have trained for years to take quick turns safely. Race car drivers have to think fast. They have to know when its safe to zoom past other drivers and when it isn't. Each driver is racing to be the first to pass under the checkered flag to victory!

What It Takes

- ✓ Fast reflexes
- ✓ Courage
- ✓ Knowledge of cars and engines
- ✓ Hours of training in cars and **simulators**

Race cars have safety harnesses to protect drivers.

24

Pit crews help drivers change tires during races.

Formula 1 race cars can get to top speeds faster than any other cars!

Race car drivers get paid a lot of money because the sport is so dangerous.

25

WHEELS FOR MILES

Long-Distance Cyclist

Professional long-distance cyclists put their bodies and bikes to the test. These cyclists ride on courses that are 20 to 2,000 miles (32 to 3,220 km) long. These courses take them around twisting streets or up steep mountains. Cycling is a sport that needs both strength and **stamina**. Riders also need **strategy**. They need to know when to ride with the group and when to break away, zooming ahead to take the lead.

What It Takes
- ☑ Knowledge of bike mechanics
- ☑ Good balance
- ☑ Endurance
- ☑ Courage

Cyclists sometimes practice on bikes that stay in one place.

Riders often stay close to those in front of them so they block the wind.

The most famous cycling race is the Tour de France. This race can cover more than 2,000 miles (3,220 km).

YOUR TURN!

People often choose a sports career because of their passion for the sport. These hard workers make games and competitions happen, so people around the world can watch and enjoy. Sports careers are a lot of work! But there's rarely a dull moment. From getting the win against another team to helping athletes stay safe, sports pros find lots of reasons to love their jobs.

SPORTS CAREER SPOTLIGHT

Mikaela Shiffrin

Mikaela Shiffrin is the most successful ski racer of all time. She has won almost 100 World Cup races—more than any other skier. Shiffrin has two Olympic gold medals and has won the overall World Championship six times in a row. Her best event is the slalom. She keeps winning because of her practice, focus, and persistence!

GLOSSARY

agility the ability to move quickly and easily

amateur taking part in sports without being paid

analysts people who study something carefully in order to understand it

anonymous not named or identified

leagues groups of teams that compete against one another

National Football League (NFL) an organization with 32 professional football teams that play against one another

plays actions performed by an athlete or team

persistence willingness to continue pushing even when things are hard

pros people who are paid to do jobs

roster a list of athletes who play on a team

slalom a type of ski race where athletes travel back and forth between closely spaced gates on a downhill track

simulators video-game-like machines that let drivers practice on virtual tracks

stamina the ability to stick with something for a long time

stat a number that shows how well a player or team is doing

strategy an overview of how a task can be accomplished

tactics the steps taken to achieve a goal

READ MORE

Arnez, Lynda. *Be a Pro Skateboarder (Go Extreme!).* New York: Gareth Stevens Publishing, 2023.

Buckley, A. W. *Jobs in Sports (Industry Jobs).* Minneapolis: Abdo Group, 2023.

Leed, Percy. *Pro Baseball by the Numbers (Ultimate Sports Stats).* Minneapolis: Lerner Publications, 2025.

LEARN MORE ONLINE

1. Go to **FactSurfer.com** or scan the QR code below.
2. Enter "**Sports Careers**" into the search box.
3. Click on the cover of this book to see a list of websites.

INDEX

announcers 21
athletic trainers 12–13
coaches 7, 18–19
cycling 26–27
Formula 1 25
free diving 14–15
mascot 10–11
NASCAR 25
National Football League (NFL) 22–23
Olympic Games 9, 17, 29
skateboarding 16–17
skiing 8–9
slalom 8, 29
Society for American Baseball Research 7
sports medicine 12
Tour de France 27
World Cup 9, 29

ABOUT THE AUTHOR

James Buckley Jr. has written more than 150 sports books for kids, including "Who Was . . . ?" biographies of Muhammad Ali, Cristiano Ronaldo, Lionel Messi, and Jim Thorpe. He also writes the annual *Scholastic Year in Sports*.